In the Year 1936

By

Kerry Butters.

In the Year 1936.

Millennium:	2nd millennium
Centuries:	19th century – **20th century** – 21st century
Decades:	1900s 1910s 1920s – **1930s** – 1940s 1950s 1960s
Years:	1933 1934 1935 – **1936** – 1937 1938 1939

1936 (MCMXXXVI) was a leap year starting on Wednesday (dominical letter ED) of the Gregorian calendar, the 1936th year of the Common Era (CE) and *Anno Domini* (AD) designations, the 936th year of the 2nd millennium, the 36th year of the 20th century, and the 7th year of the 1930s decade.

Contents

Events

January

- January 4 – England celebrates its first ever win over the All Blacks in rugby union, in particular the two famous tries by "The Prince" HH Alexander Obolensky.
- January 11 – *I Wanna Play House* marks the first Warner Bros. cartoon with "target"
- January 15 – The first building to be completely covered in glass is completed in Toledo, Ohio, for the Owens-Illinois Glass Company.
- January 16 – Serial killer Albert Fish is executed in Sing Sing Prison.
- January 20 – King George V of the United Kingdom dies. His eldest son succeeds to the throne, becoming Edward VIII. The title Prince of Wales is not used for another 22 years.
- January 31 – *The Green Hornet* radio show debuts.

February

- February – John Maynard Keynes' book *The General Theory of Employment, Interest and Money* is published in the UK.
- February 4 – Radium E (bismuth-210) becomes the first radioactive element to be made synthetically.
- February 6 – The IV Olympic Winter Games open in Garmisch-Partenkirchen, Germany.
- February 10–19 – Second Italo-Ethiopian War: Battle of Amba Aradam in Ethiopia, ending in a decisive tactical victory for Italian forces, effectively neutralizing the army of the Ethiopian Empire.
- February 17 – The first superhero to wear a skin-tight costume and mask, *The Phantom*, makes his first appearance in U.S. newspapers.
- February 26 – February 26 Incident (二・二六事件, *Niniroku Jiken*): The Imperial Way Faction engineers a failed coup against the Japanese government; some politicians are killed.
- February 29 – Emperor Hirohito orders the Japanese army to arrest 123 conspirators in Tokyo government offices; 19 of them are executed in July.

March

March 1: Hoover Dam is completed

- March 1 – Construction of Hoover Dam is completed in the United States.
- March 7 – In violation of the Treaty of Versailles and Locarno Treaties, Nazi Germany reoccupies the Rhineland. According to several historians, like Samuel Mitcham, this is the last time when the Allies could have stopped Hitler with the odds overwhelmingly on their side. Hitler and other Nazis admit that the French army alone could have destroyed the Wehrmacht.
- March 9 – Pro-democratic militarist Keisuke Okada steps down as Prime Minister of Japan and is replaced by radical militarist Kōki Hirota.
- March 17–18 – Pittsburgh Flood of 1936 ("Saint Patrick's Day Flood"): Pittsburgh, Pennsylvania, suffers the worst flooding in its history.
- March 26 – The longest game in the history of the National Hockey League is played when the Montreal Maroons and Detroit Red Wings go scoreless until 16 and a half minutes into the sixth OT when Mud Bruneteau ends it at 2:25 in the morning.

April

- April 3 – Richard Hauptmann, convicted of the Lindbergh kidnapping and murder in 1932, is executed by electrocution in New Jersey State Prison.
- April 5 – A tornado hits Tupelo, Mississippi, killing 216 and injuring over 700 (the 4th deadliest tornado in U.S. history).

- April 6 – Two tornadoes strike Gainesville, Georgia. The smaller tornado hits north Gainesville, the stronger tornado the west side of town. 203 die and 1,600 are injured in the 5th deadliest tornado in U.S. history.
- April 11 – Billy Butlin opens his first Butlins holiday camp, Butlins Skegness, in Skegness (Ingoldmells), Lincolnshire, England. It is officially opened by Amy Johnson of Hull (the first woman to fly solo from England to Australia).
- April 19 – The 1936–39 Arab revolt in Palestine against the British government and opposition to Jewish immigration begins.

May

- May 2 – *Peter and the Wolf*, a Russian fairy tale of Sergei Prokofiev's composition, debuts at the Nezlobin Theater in Moscow, Soviet Union.
- May 5 – Italian forces occupy Addis Ababa.
- May 7 – Italy annexes Ethiopia.
- May 9 – Italian East Africa is formed from the Italian territories of Eritrea, Ethiopia, and Italian Somaliland.
- May 12 – The Santa Fe railroad in the United States inaugurates the all-Pullman *Super Chief* passenger train between Chicago and Los Angeles.
- May 25 – The Remington Rand strike of 1936–37 begins, spawning the notorious "Mohawk Valley formula", a corporate plan for strikebreaking.
- May 27
  - The first flight by the Irish airline Aer Lingus takes place.

- British luxury liner RMS *Queen Mary* leaves Southampton on her maiden voyage across the Atlantic.
- May 28 – Alan Turing submits his paper "On Computable Numbers" to the London Mathematical Society for publication, introducing the concept of the "Turing machine". Its formal publication is on November 12.

June

- June
  - A major heat wave strikes North America; high temperature records are set and thousands die.
  - The first production model PCC streetcar, built by St. Louis Car Company, is placed in service by Pittsburgh Railways.
- June 7
  - The general strike in France is ended by the Matignon Agreements.
  - The Steel Workers Organizing Committee is founded in the United States.
- June 10 – Margaret Mitchell's epic historical romance *Gone with the Wind* is first published in the United States.
- June 15 – An army ammunition depot explosion kills 60 in Männiku, Estonia.
- June 19 – Max Schmeling knocks out Joe Louis in the 12th round of their heavyweight boxing match at Yankee Stadium in New York City.
- June 19 – Per Albin Hansson resigns as Prime Minister of Sweden, over the issue of defence policy. He is replaced by

the leader of the Farmer's League (*Bondeförbundet*) Axel Pehrsson-Bramstorp , whom also becomes Minister of Agriculture.

- June 26 – Focke-Wulf Fw 61, the first fully controllable helicopter, makes its maiden flight.
- June 29 – United States Maritime Commission is formed.

July

- July 11 – The Triborough Bridge in New York City is opened to traffic – the bridge was renamed Robert F. Kennedy Bridge in 2008.
- July 13 – 14 – Peak of July 1936 heat wave: The U.S. states of Wisconsin, Michigan, and Indiana all set new state records for high temperature. At Mio in northern Michigan, it soars to 113 °F (45 °C).
- July 17 – The Spanish Army of Africa launches a *coup d'état* against the Second Spanish Republic, beginning the Spanish Civil War.
- July 20 – Montreux Convention Regarding the Regime of the Straits is signed in Montreux, allowing Turkey to fortify the Dardanelles and the Bosphorus but guaranteeing free passage to ships of all nations in peacetime.

August

- August 1 – The 1936 Summer Olympics open in Berlin, Germany, and mark the first live television coverage of a sports event in world history. Note that John Logie Baird had previously broadcast the Derby horse race in Britain in 1931.

- August 3 – African-American athlete Jesse Owens wins the 100-meter dash at the Berlin Olympics.
- August 14
  - Rainey Bethea was hanged in Owensboro, Kentucky, in the last public execution in the United States
  - 1936 Summer Olympics: The United States men's national basketball team wins the first Olympic basketball tournament in the final game over Canada, 19–8.
- August 19 – The first of the Moscow Trials begins in the Soviet Union.
- August 26 – Anglo-Egyptian Treaty of 1936 is signed.
- August 30
  - Ernest Nash flees Germany for Rome.
  - President Franklin D. Roosevelt attends the dedication of Thomas Jefferson's head at Mount Rushmore.

September

- September 4–5 – English-born aviatrix Beryl Markham becomes the first woman to make an East-to-West solo transatlantic flight, from Abingdon-on-Thames, England, to Baleine, Nova Scotia.
- September 5 – Spanish Civil War: Robert Capa's photograph *The Falling Soldier* is taken.
- September 7 – The last known thylacine (Tasmanian Tiger), named Benjamin, dies in Hobart Zoo in Tasmania.
- September 9
  - The crews of Portuguese Navy frigate *NRP Afonso de Albuquerque* and destroyer *Dão* mutinied while

anchored in Lisbon harbour. Opposed to the Salazar dictatorship's support of General Franco's coup, they declared their solidarity with the Spanish Republic.

- The Franco-Syrian Treaty of Independence is signed.
- September 10 – The first World Speedway Championship is held at Wembley Stadium in London, England. It is won by Australian Lionel Van Praag, with Englishman Eric Langton second and Australian Bluey Wilkinson third.
- September 12 – The Walt Disney animated short *Donald and Pluto* is released.
- September 28 – After the election to the Swedish Riksdag`s second chamber, Axel Pehrsson-Bramstorp (but remains as Minister of Agriculture) and his "Holiday Cabinet" (*"Semesterregeringen"*) resigns. Per Albin Hansson returns as Prime Minister, and stays in office to his death in a heart attack in 1946 .

October

- October – Start of Joseph Stalin's Great Purge in the Soviet Union.
  - The Mästermyr chest is discovered in the Mästermyr mire (after which it is later named) west of Hemse on the island of Gotland, Sweden.
- October 11 – Earl Bascom, rodeo cowboy and artist, designs and builds Mississippi's first permanent rodeo arena at Columbia, Mississippi.
- October 19 – H.R. Ekins, reporter for the *New York World-Telegram*, wins a race to travel around the world on commercial airline flights, beating Dorothy Kilgallen of the

New York Journal and Leo Kieran of the *New York Times*. The flight takes 18½ days.

- October 25 – Rome-Berlin Axis is formed.
- October 29 – The historic Uptown Theater (Washington, D.C.) opens.

Family during the Great Depression, Oklahoma, 1936

November

- November 2
  - The BBC launches the world's first regular (then) high-definition television service.
  - The Canadian Broadcasting Corporation (CBC) begins radio in Canada.
- November 3 – U.S. presidential election, 1936: Franklin D. Roosevelt is reelected to a second term in a landslide victory over Kansas Governor Alf Landon. Farmers support Roosevelt.
- November 9 – American fashion designer Ruth Harkness encounters and captures a nine-week-old panda cub in Sichuan, China; it becomes the first live giant panda to enter the United States.

- November 12 – In California, the San Francisco–Oakland Bay Bridge opens to traffic.
- November 20 – A levee failure and continued massive rain at the Mitsubishi Osarizawa mine, Kazuno, northeastern Akita, Japan, results in at least 375 deaths.
- November 23 – This is the cover date of the first issue of *Life*, a weekly news magazine in the United States under the management of Henry Luce.
- November 26 – The Anti-Comintern Pact is signed by Germany and Japan.
- November 30 – In London, the Crystal Palace is destroyed in a fire (it had been built for the 1851 Great Exhibition).

December

- December 1 – Hitler mandates that all German boys aged 10 to 18 join the Hitler Youth paramilitary organization.
- December 3 – Radio station WQXR is officially founded in New York City.
- December 5 – 1936 Soviet Constitution, promulgated by Stalin, is adopted in the Soviet Union. The Transcaucasian Socialist Federative Soviet Republic is dissolved and Armenia, Azerbaijan, and Georgia become full Republics of the Soviet Union.
- December 10 – Edward VIII abdication crisis: King Edward VIII of the United Kingdom signs an instrument of abdication at Fort Belvedere, Surrey in the presence of his three brothers, The Duke of York, The Duke of Gloucester and The Duke of Kent.
- December 11 – Edward VIII abdication crisis:

- The British Parliament passes His Majesty's Declaration of Abdication Act 1936 on behalf of the U.K., Australia, New Zealand and South Africa. The King performs his last act as sovereign by giving Royal Assent to the Act, and his brother Prince Albert, Duke of York, becomes King, reigning as King George VI.
- The abdicated King Edward VIII, now HRH Prince Edward, makes a broadcast to the nation explaining his decision to abdicate. He leaves the country for Austria.
- Taking the opportunity to free itself further from ties to the United Kingdom, the Oireachtas of the Irish Free State passes the Constitution (Amendment No. 27) Act 1936, removing most powers from the office of Governor-General of the Irish Free State, and the Executive Authority (External Relations) Act 1936 (signed into law December 12) assenting to the abdication and restricting the power of the monarch in relation to Ireland to international affairs.

- December 12 – Xi'an Incident: Generalissimo Chiang Kai-shek of the Republic of China is kidnapped by Marshal Zhang Xueliang.
- December 24 – Release of the film *Natalka Poltavka* in Ukraine, the first filmed Russian opera.
- December 26 – The Abraham Lincoln Brigade sails from New York City on its way to the Spanish Civil War.
- December 30 – The United Auto Workers begins the Flint Sit-Down Strike in Flint, Michigan.

Date unknown

- West China Famine: five million die.
- Ipswich Town Football Club turns professional.
- The YMCA Youth and Government program is founded in Albany, New York.
- Mordecai Ham begins his radio ministry.
- Stress is first recognised as a medical condition.
- Polaroid sunglasses and Ambre Solaire sunblock both first marketed.
- Cocoa production in the Gold Coast reaches 305,000 tons.

Births

January

Émile Lahoud

- January 2 – Roger Miller, American singer (d. 1992)
- January 5 – Florence King, American writer (d. 2016)
- January 6

- ○ Nida Blanca, Filipina actress (d. 2001)
- ○ Julio María Sanguinetti Coirolo, President of Uruguay
- January 10
  - ○ Stephen Ambrose, American historian (d. 2002)
  - ○ Burnum Burnum, Australian Aboriginal activist, author and actor (d. 1997)
  - ○ Robert Wilson, American physicist and radio astronomer, Nobel Prize laureate
- January 11 – Eva Hesse, American artist (d. 1970)
- January 12 – Émile Lahoud, President of Lebanon
- January 14 – Reiner Klimke, German equestrian (d. 1999)
- January 20 – The Honourable Frances Shand Kydd, mother of Princess Diana (d. 2004)
- January 23
  - ○ Arlene Golonka, American actress
  - ○ Jerry Kramer, American football player
- January 27 – Troy Donahue, American actor (d. 2001)
- January 28
  - ○ Alan Alda, American actor
  - ○ Ismail Kadare, Albanian writer
- January 29
  - ○ Patrick Caulfield, English artist (d. 2005)
  - ○ James Jamerson, American bass guitarist for Motown Records (d. 1983)

February

Burt Reynolds

- February 3
  - Jim Marshall, American photographer (d. 2010)
  - Elizabeth Peer, American journalist (d. 1984)
- February 4
  - David Brenner, American comedian (d. 2014)
  - Gary Conway, American actor
- February 6 – Kent Douglas, Canadian ice hockey player and coach (d. 2009)
- February 8 – Larry Verne, American singer and songwriter (d. 2013)
- February 9
  - Stompin' Tom Connors, Canadian country/folk singer (d. 2013)
  - Clive Swift, British actor
- February 11 – Burt Reynolds, American actor
- February 14 – Andrew Prine, American actor
- February 17 – Jim Brown, African-American football player
- February 19 – Sam Myers, American musician and songwriter (d. 2006)
- February 20

- ○ Larry Hovis, American actor (*Hogan's Heroes*) (d. 2003)
- ○ Shigeo Nagashima, Japanese professional baseball player and coach
- February 22 – Elizabeth MacRae, American actress
- February 24 – Lance Reventlow, English playboy, entrepreneur, and race car driver (d. 1972)
- February 27 – Roger Cardinal Mahony, fourth Archbishop of Los Angeles
- February 29 – Alex Rocco, American actor (d. 2015)

March

Sepp Blatter

F. W. De Klerk

Ursula Andress

- March 2 – Alan Scott, blacksmith and brick oven constructor (d. 2009)
- March 4
  - Jim Clark, Scottish race car driver (d. 1968)
  - Aribert Reimann, German composer
- March 5 – Dean Stockwell, American actor
- March 6
  - Marion Barry, Mayor of Washington, D.C. (d. 2014)
  - Elmira Zherzdeva, Soviet singer and voice actress
- March 7
  - Loren Acton, American astronaut
  - Julio Terrazas Sandoval, Bolivian cardinal (d. 2015)
- March 8 – Sue Ane Langdon, American actress
- March 9
  - Mickey Gilley, American musician
  - Tom Sestak, American football player (d. 1987)
- March 10 – Sepp Blatter, president of FIFA
- March 11 – Antonin Scalia, U.S. Supreme Court Justice (d. 2016)
- March 15 – Howard Greenfield, American songwriter (d. 1986)

- March 16
    - Raymond Vahan Damadian, Armenian-American MRI practitioner
    - Elisabeth Volkmann, German actress (d. 2006)
- March 17 – Patty Maloney, American actress
- March 18 – F. W. de Klerk, President of South Africa (1989–94); 7th and last head of state of South Africa under the apartheid era.
- March 19 – Ursula Andress, Swiss actress
- March 20 – Lee "Scratch" Perry, Jamaican musician
- March 24 – Don Covay, American singer and songwriter (d. 2015)
- March 26 – Harry Kalas, American sportscaster (d. 2009)
- March 28 – Mario Vargas Llosa, Peruvian writer, politician, journalist, essayist and Nobel Prize laureate
- March 31 – Marge Piercy, American poet and activist

April

Roy Orbison

- April 9 – Valerie Solanas, American feminist and writer who attempted to kill Andy Warhol (d. 1988)
- April 10
    - John Howell, British long jumper

- John Madden, American football coach and television sportscaster
- Bobby Smith, American singer and songwriter (d. 2013)
- April 12 – Charles Napier, American actor (d. 2011)
- April 14 – Kenneth Mars, American actor (d. 2011)
- April 17 – Jiří Grygar, Czech astronomer
- April 21 – James Dobson, American child psychologist and conservative political activist (*Focus On The Family*)
- April 22
  - Glen Campbell, American country musician
  - Dieter Kronzucker, German journalist and television presenter
- April 23 – Roy Orbison, American singer-songwriter (d. 1988)
- April 24
  - Glen Hobbie, American baseball player (d. 2013)
  - Jill Ireland, English actress (d. 1990)
- April 28 – Tariq Aziz, Iraqi political (d. 2015)

May

Dennis Hopper

- May 1 – Danièle Huillet, French filmmaker (d. 2006)
- May 2
  - Sam DeLuca, American football offensive lineman and sports broadcaster (d. 2011)

- Engelbert Humperdinck, British singer
  - Perdita Huston, American journalist (d. 2001)
  - Norma Aleandro, Argentinian actress
- May 4 – Ludwig von Falkenhausen, German general (b. 1844)
- May 7 – Jimmy Ruffin, American singer (d. 2014)
- May 9
  - Albert Finney, English actor
  - Glenda Jackson, British actress and politician
- May 12
  - Guillermo Endara, President of Panama (1989–1994) (d. 2009)
  - Tom Snyder, American talk show host (*Tomorrow*) (d. 2007)
  - Frank Stella, American minimalist painter
- May 14
  - Bobby Darin, American singer (d. 1973)
  - Dick Howser, American baseball shortstop/manager (d. 1987)
- May 15
  - Wavy Gravy, American anti-war activist
  - Paul Zindel, American writer (d. 2003)
- May 17 – Dennis Hopper, American actor and director (d. 2010)
- May 23 – Ingeborg Hallstein, German opera singer
- May 25 – Tom T. Hall, American country singer

June

Bruce Dern

Kris Kristofferson

- June 4 – Bruce Dern, American actor
- June 8 – James Darren, American actor and singer
- June 12 – Marcus Belgrave, American jazz trumpeter (d. 2015)
- June 17 – Ken Loach, British director
- June 18
    - Ronald Runaldo Venetiaan, President of Suriname
    - Dick Wimmer, American novelist (d. 2011)
- June 19 – Takeshi Aono, Japanese voice actor (d. 2012)
- June 20 – Harold E. Puthoff, American physicist
- June 21 – Joseph Gosnell, Nisga'a statesman
- June 22 – Kris Kristofferson, American actor, singer-songwriter

- June 25 – Bacharuddin Jusuf Habibie, 3rd President of Indonesia
- June 26 – Jean-Claude Turcotte, Canadian cardinal (d. 2015)
- June 27 – Joe Doyle, Irish politician (d. 2009)
- June 28 – Chuck Howley, American football player
- June 29 – Harmon Killebrew, American baseball player (d. 2011)
- June 29 – Eddie Mabo, Australian Indigenous rights activist (d. 1992)
- June 30 – Assia Djebar, Algerian writer (d. 2015)

July

Shirley Knight

- July 2 – Rex Gildo, German singer
- July 5 – Shirley Knight, American actress
- July 8 – Tony Warren, English television screenwriter (d. 2016)
- July 9
  - André Pronovost, Canadian ice hockey player
  - Richard Wilson, Scottish actor and director
- July 10
  - Herbert Boyer, Biotechnology entrepreneur
  - Tunne Kelam, Estonian politician

- July 15 – George Voinovich, American politician; United States Senator (R-OH)
- July 16
  - Yasuo Fukuda, 58th Prime Minister of Japan
  - Buddy Merrill, American musician (*The Lawrence Welk Show*)
- July 18 – Ted Harris, Canadian ice hockey player
- July 20 – Barbara Mikulski, American politician; United States Senator (D-MD)
- July 22 – Klaus Bresser, German journalist and television presenter
- July 23 – Don Drysdale, American baseball player (d. 1993)
- July 24
  - Ruth Buzzi, American actress and comedian
  - Mark Goddard, American actor and teacher
- July 26 – Mary Millar, British actress (d. 1998)
- July 28 – Russ Jackson, Canadian football player
- July 29 – Elizabeth Dole, U.S. Senator from North Carolina
- July 30
  - Buddy Guy, American blues guitarist and singer
  - Ted Rogers, English comedian and game show host (d. 2001)

August

Robert Redford

Wilt Chamberlain

John McCain

- August 1
  - Bradford Bishop, American fugitive
  - Donald Neilson, British serial killer (d. 2011)

- Yves Saint Laurent, Algerian-born French fashion designer (d. 2008)
- August 6 – Robert Gnaizda, lawyer and social justice advocate
- August 11 – Andre Dubus, American short-story writer (d. 1999)
- August 12
  - André Kolingba, President of Central African Republic (d. 2010)
  - Tom McAvoy, American baseball player (d. 2011)
- August 18 – Robert Redford, American actor
- August 21 – Wilt Chamberlain, African-American basketball player (d. 1999)
- August 24 – Kenny Guinn, American politician (d. 2010)
- August 25 – Giridharilal Kedia, Former Working President of KVK (d. 2009)
- August 26 – Benedict Anderson, American academic (d. 2015)
- August 29 – John McCain, U.S. Senator from Arizona; 2008 Republican Presidential candidate

September

Zine El-Abidine Ben Ali

Jim Henson

Silvio Berlusconi

Brian Blessed

Václav Havel

Bill Wyman

- September 2
    - Andrew Grove, Hungarian-American businessman, engineer and author (d. 2016)
    - Károly Krajczár, Hungarian Slovene teacher, writer and collector
- September 3 – Zine El Abidine Ben Ali, 2nd President of Tunisia
- September 7 – Buddy Holly, American rock 'n' roll singer (d. 1959)
- September 11 – Charles Dierkop, American actor
- September 14 – Walter Koenig, American actor (*Star Trek*)
- September 19 – Anna Karen, British actress

- September 21 – Yury Luzhkov, mayor of Moscow
- September 24 – Jim Henson, American puppeteer, filmmaker, and television producer (d. 1990)
- September 25
  - Ken Forsse, American inventor and producer, creator of Teddy Ruxpin (d. 2014)
  - Moussa Traoré, President of Mali
- September 27
  - Don Cornelius, African-American television personality (d. 2012)
  - Joselo, Venezuelan actor and comedian (d. 2013)
- September 29 – Silvio Berlusconi, Italian Prime Minister, media entrepreneur

October

- October 1 – Duncan Edwards, English footballer (d. 1958)
- October 3 – Steve Reich, American composer
- October 5 – Václav Havel, Czech playwright, writer and politician (d. 2011)
- October 7 – Fereydoun Farrokhzad, Iranian entertainer (d. 1992)
- October 9 – Brian Blessed, English actor
- October 10 – Gerhard Ertl, German physicist, Nobel Prize laureate
- October 11 – Larry Staverman, American professional basketball player and coach (d. 2007)
- October 13 – Christine Nöstlinger, Austrian writer
- October 14 – Carrie Nye, American actress (d. 2006)
- October 19

- James Bevel, American civil rights activist (d. 2008)
- Tony Lo Bianco, American actor
- October 24
  - David Nelson, American actor and singer (d. 2011)
  - Bill Wyman, British musician (The Rolling Stones)
- October 25
  - Martin Gilbert, British historian (d. 2015)
  - Masako Nozawa, Japanese voice actress
- October 26 – Shelley Morrison, American actress
  - Etelka Kenéz Heka, Hungarian writer, poet, singer
- October 29 – Akiko Kojima, Japanese model
- October 31 – Michael Landon, American actor and director (d. 1991)

November

David Carradine

Pope Francis

- November 2 – Rose Bird, American judge (d. 1999)
- November 3 – Roy Emerson, Australian tennis player
- November 4 – C. K. Williams, American poet
- November 5
    - Uwe Seeler, German football player and manager
    - Billy Sherrill, American record producer, arranger and songwriter (d. 2015)
- November 8 – Virna Lisi, Italian actress (d. 2014)
- November 9 – Teddy Infuhr, American child actor (d. 2007)
- November 15 – Wolf Biermann, German singer-songwriter and former East German dissident
- November 19 – Dick Cavett, American talk show host and television personality
- November 20 – Don DeLillo, American author
- November 23
    - Robert Barnard, British writer, critic and lecturer (d. 2013)
    - Steve Landesberg, American actor and director (d. 2010)
- November 27 – Dahlia Ravikovitch, Israeli poet (d. 2005)

December

- December 5 – James Lee Burke, American writer
- December 6 – Kenneth Copeland, American televangelist
- December 8
    - David Carradine, American actor, director, martial artist (d. 2009)
    - Michael Hobson, American publisher

- December 12 – Iolanda Balaș, Romanian high jumper (d. 2016)
- December 15 – Donald Goines, American novelist (d. 1973)
- December 17
  - Pope Francis
  - Klaus Kinkel, German politician
- December 22
  - James Burke, British broadcaster, science historian, author and television producer
  - Héctor Elizondo, American actor
- December 23 – James Stacy, American actor
- December 25 – Princess Alexandra, The Honourable Lady Ogilvy, British aristocrat and socialite; youngest granddaughter of King George V and Queen Mary
- December 29 – Mary Tyler Moore, American actress, producer, diabetes awareness activist
- December 31
- Siw Malmkvist, Swedish singer
  - Szilveszter E. Vizi, Hungarian physician, neuroscientist and pharmacologist

Date unknown

- Dolores Mantez, British actress (d. 2012)

Deaths

January

George V of the United Kingdom

Charles Curtis

Fuad I of Egypt

- January 1 – Harry B. Smith, American composer (b. 1860)
- January 4 – James Churchward, British writer (b. 1851)

- January 5 – Ramón del Valle-Inclán, Spanish writer (b. 1866)
- January 6 – Louise Bryant, American journalist (b. 1885)
- January 9 – John Gilbert, American actor (b. 1899)
- January 15
  - Henry Foster, British Conservative Party politician, former Governor-General of Australia (b. 1866)
  - George Landenberger, United States Navy Captain and the 23rd Governor of American Samoa (b. 1879)
- January 16 – Albert Fish, American serial killer (b. 1870)
- January 18 – Rudyard Kipling, British writer, Nobel Prize laureate (b. 1865)
- January 20 – King George V of the United Kingdom (b. 1865)
- January 23 – John Mills, Jr., "Mills Brothers" basso and guitarist (b. 1911)
- January 24 – Harry Peach, British furniture manufacturer and social campaigner (b. 1874)
- January 28 – Richard Loeb, American murderer (b. 1905)

February

- February 3 – Princess Sophie of Schönburg-Waldenburg, consort of William of Wied, Prince of Albania (b.1885)
- February 4 – Wilhelm Gustloff, German leader of the Swiss Nazi Party (b. 1895)
- February 8 – Charles Curtis, 31st Vice President of the United States (b. 1860)
- February 19 – Billy Mitchell, U.S. general and military aviation pioneer (b. 1879)
- February 20 – Georges Vacher de Lapouge, French anthropologist (b. 1854)

- February 23 – William Adamson, British Labour politician (b. 1863)
- February 26 – in the "February 26 Incident":
  - Takahashi Korekiyo, 11th Prime Minister of Japan (b. 1854)
  - Saitō Makoto, Japanese admiral, 19th Prime Minister of Japan (b. 1858)
- February 27
  - Ivan Pavlov, Russian psychologist, recipient of the Nobel Prize in Physiology or Medicine (b. 1849)
  - Mulugeta Yeggazu, Ethiopian government official and military leader
- February 28 – Charles Nicolle, French bacteriologist, recipient of the Nobel Prize in Physiology or Medicine (b. 1866)

March

- March 11 – David Beatty, 1st Earl Beatty, British admiral (b. 1871)
- March 16 – Marguerite Durand, French journalist and feminist leader (b. 1864)
- March 18 – Eleftherios Venizelos, Greek Statesman, several times Prime Minister (b. 1864)
- March 21 – Alexander Glazunov, Russian composer and conductor (b. 1865)
- March 23 – Oscar Asche, Australian actor (b. 1871)
- March 28 – Archibald Garrod, English physician (b. 1857)

April

- April 2 – Alberico Albricci, Italian general (b. 1864)
- April 3 – Bruno Richard Hauptmann, German killer of Charles Lindbergh, Jr. (executed) (b. 1899)
- April 7 – Marilyn Miller, American actress (b. 1898)
- April 8 – Róbert Bárány, Austrian physician, recipient of the Nobel Prize in Physiology or Medicine (b. 1876)
- April 18 – Ottorino Respighi, Italian composer, musicologist, and conductor (b. 1879)
- April 23 – Teresa de la Parra, Venezuelan writer (b. 1889)
- April 26 – Tammany Young, American actor (b. 1886)
- April 28 – Fuad I of Egypt, King of Egypt (b. 1868)
- April 30 – Alfred Edward Housman, English poet (b. 1859)

May

- May 4 – Ludwig von Falkenhausen, German general (b. 1844)
- May 8 – Oswald Spengler, German philosopher (b. 1880)
- May 14 – Edmund Allenby, 1st Viscount Allenby, British soldier and administrator (b. 1861)
- May 16 – Leonidas Paraskevopoulos, Greek general and senator (b. 1860)
- May 20 – Elmer Fowler Stone, American aviator, the first United States Coast Guard aviator (b. 1887)
- May 29 – Norman Chaney, American actor (b. 1914)

June

- June 3 – Walther Wever, German general and *Luftwaffe* commander (b. 1887)
- June 11 – Robert E. Howard, American author (suicide) (b. 1906)
- June 12 – Karl Krays, Austrian writer and journalist, (b. 1874)
- June 14 – G. K. Chesterton, English author (b. 1874)
- June 17 – Henry B. Walthall, American actor (b. 1878)
- June 18 – Maxim Gorky, Russian writer (b. 1868)
- June 22 – Moritz Schlick, German philosopher and physicist (b. 1882)
- June 28 – Alexander Berkman Russian anarchist (b. 1870)
- June 29 – János Szlepecz Slovene priest and writer (b. 1872)

July

Arvid Lindman

- July 8 – Thomas Meighan, American actor (b. 1879)
- July 11 – James Murray, American actor (b. 1901)
- July 13 – José Calvo Sotelo, Spanish politician (b. 1893)
- July 16 – Alan Crosland, American film director (b. 1894)
- July 20 – José Sanjurjo, Spanish general (b. 1872)

- July 24 – Georg Michaelis, former Chancellor of Germany (b. 1857)

August

- August 1 – Louis Blériot, French aviation pioneer (b. 1872)
- August 9 – Lincoln Steffens, American journalist (b. 1866)
- August 12 – Blessed Victoria Díez Bustos de Molina, Spanish teacher and religious woman (b. 1903)
- August 15 – Grazia Deledda, Italian writer, Nobel Prize laureate (b. 1871)
- August 19
  - Federico García Lorca, Spanish writer (b. 1898)
  - Hugh Patrick Lygon, English aristocrat (b. 1904)
- August 25
  - Ivan Nikitich Smirnov, Communist Party activist (b. 1881)
  - Lev Kamenev, Soviet politician (b. 1883)
  - Grigory Zinoviev, Soviet politician (b. 1883)

September

- September 7 – Kenneth Robert Balfour, British Conservative Party politician (b. 1863)
- September 14 – Irving Thalberg, American film producer (b. 1899)
- September 16 – Karl Buresch, 10th Chancellor of Austria (b. 1878)
- September 17 – Henri Louis Le Chatelier, French chemist (Le Chatelier's principle) (b. 1850)

- September 19 – Vishnu Narayan Bhatkhande, Indian musician (b. 1860)
- September 21 – Antoine Meillet, French linguist (b. 1866)
- September 24 – József Klekl, Slovene writer and journalist (b. 1879)
- September 25 – William Sims, American admiral (b. 1858)
- September 30 – Friedrich Sixt von Armin, German general (b. 1851)

October

- October 2 – Juho Sunila, twice Prime Minister of Finland (b. 1875)
- October 3 – John Heisman, American football coach (b. 1869)
- October 8
  - Cheiro, Irish astrologer (b. 1866)
  - William Henry Stark, American businessman (b. 1851)
- October 20 – Anne Sullivan, American teacher of Helen Keller (b. 1866)
- October 26 – Rodney Heath, Australian tennis player (b. 1884)
- October 29 – Ramiro de Maeztu, Spanish writer (b. 1875)

November

- November 7 – Chic Sale, American vaudevillian (b. 1885)
- November 17 – John Bowers, American actor (b. 1885)
- November 20 – Buenaventura Durruti, Spanish anarchist (b. 1896)
- November 20 – José Antonio Primo de Rivera, Spanish fascist politician (b. 1903)

- November 25 – Andrew Harper, Scottish–Australian biblical scholar and teacher (b. 1844)
- November 27 – Edward Bach, British physician, homeopath and bacteriologist (b. 1886)

December

- December 9
  - Juan de la Cierva, Spanish civil engineer, aviator, aeronautical engineer, inventor of the autogyro (b. 1895)
  - Arvid Lindman, 12th Prime Minister of Sweden (b. 1862)
  - Lottie Pickford, Canadian actress (b. 1895)
- December 10
  - Bobby Abel, English cricketer (b. 1857)
  - Luigi Pirandello, Italian writer, Nobel Prize laureate (b. 1867)
- December 11 – Myron Grimshaw, American baseball player (b. 1875)
- December 18 – Leonardo Torres y Quevedo, Spanish engineer and mathematician (b. 1852)
- December 23 – William Henry Harrison, English cricketer (b. 1866)
- December 24 – Irene Fenwick, American actress (b. 1887)
- December 25 – Carl Stumpf, German philosopher and psychologist (b. 1848)
- December 27 – Hans von Seeckt, German general (b. 1866)
- December 29 – Lucy, Lady Houston, British philanthropist (b. 1857)

Nobel Prizes

- Physics – Victor F. Hess, Carl D. Anderson
- Chemistry – Petrus (Peter) Josephus Wilhelmus Debye
- Physiology or Medicine – Sir Henry Hallett Dale, Otto Loewi
- Literature – Eugene Gladstone O'Neill
- Peace – Carlos Saavedra Lamas

In the News.

King Edward VIII abdicates to marry Wallis Simpson.

The Summer Olympics are held in Berlin, Germany.

Jesse Owens wins 4 Gold medals on August 9th at the Summer Olympics in Berlin.

BBC starts the first public Television broadcasts in London.

On July 18th The Spanish Civil War begins.

The book Gone With The Wind is Published on June 30th.

President Roosevelt is re-elected for a second term.

The Winter Olympic Games are held in Garmisch-Partenkirchen, Germany.

Popular films - The Alamo,The Great Ziegfeld,The Charge of the Light Brigade,Follow the Fleet, starring Fred Astaire.

Germany Breaks Treaty of Versailles.

Hoover Dam finished and begins creating hydroelectric power.

Cunard Ocean liner The Queen Mary begins Atlantic crossings.

The German airship "The Hindenburg" had its first public flight during March of 1936.

The British Air Ministry orders 310 Spitfire Fighter aircraft.

Killer Tornadoes strike Tupelo, Mississippi and Gainesville, Georgia.

The Crystal Palace Is Destroyed By Fire **on November 30th.**

The Tasmanian Tiger or Tasmanian Wolf became extinct.

Inventions – The Helicopter, Zippo Lighter, Magnetic Recording Tape.

Billboard Magazine publishes the first pop music chart.